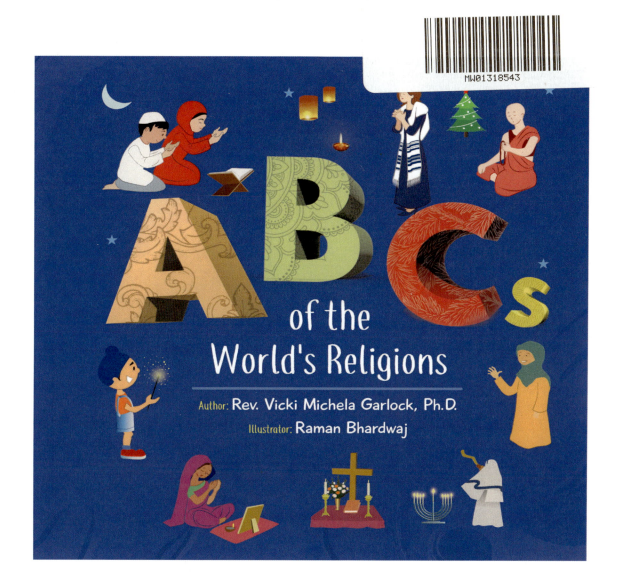

ABCs of the World's Religions

Author: Rev. Vicki Michela Garlock, Ph.D.
Illustrator: Raman Bhardwaj

Copyright © 2023 Rev. Vicki Michela Garlock, Ph.D.

ISBN: 978-1-947486-27-0

All rights reserved. No part of this publication may be reproduced, stored in a retrieval system, or transmitted in any form or by any means, electronic, mechanical, photocopying, recording, scanning, or otherwise, without the prior written approval of the author.

Published and distributed by

Eaton Press
We Make Your Book Happen

EatonPress.com
Murrells Inlet, SC

To Tony and Mariah McKinney

who just found out that a poster

in the bathroom of their beach house

inspired this book

Welcome

Thank you for choosing to share the world's faith traditions with the young people in your life. We hope this book will offer insights for both you and them!

As you will see, each letter is given a two-page spread. The left-hand pages read somewhat like a board book and use rhyming couplets, so even very young children can enjoy them. The right-hand pages offer further (non-rhyming) exploration. Sometimes, I simply provide additional information. But, where appropriate, I try to share commonalities across religious traditions. A few of them might be a bit surprising!

I have also included pronunciation guides for words that might be unfamiliar. Rather than using the International Phonetic Alphabet, which can be hard to decipher, I've used simple English-based transcriptions. Pronunciations are not as straight-forward as they might seem. They often vary across sect, denomination, country, and geographical region. Also, the multi-syllabic words found in many Asian traditions are frequently said with no clearly-accented syllable, which can be difficult for English-speakers to reproduce. So, just do your best!! Mispronunciations are not crimes, or even sins, in any faith tradition.

The variability in pronunciation is also reflected in how words are spelled. This is especially true when writing out sounds/letters that don't really exist in the English language. For example, the Buddhist holiday of Vesak, which is used for the letter V in this book, is also frequently spelled with a W. In most cases, I've chosen to use the Wikipedia spelling. Wikipedia is certainly not a go-to resource for academic scholars, but entries often include common alternate pronunciations/spellings and, for non-scholars, it can be a great place to start your own "research."

Fortunately, kids do not care much about pronunciations or spellings, so just enjoy the book. We have much to learn from our fellow humans and the wisdom of our ancestors. And, while we obviously need to be respectful of others' religious belief systems, it's completely acceptable to delight in learning about them! I am always happy to hear from my readers and/or to answer questions. I am on several social media platforms, including Facebook (WorldReligions4Kids), Twitter (WorldRel4Kids), Instagram (WorldReligions4Kids), and TikTok (@LearnReligions).

A is for ALTARS
that hold special things.
Flowers, candles, and books,
along with other offerings

Altars were some of the first sacred spaces humans ever built. They are found in many religious settings, including Hindu and Buddhist temples and Christian churches. Incense, water bowls, and money are other common altar items.

B is for the BUDDHA
who lived very long ago.
He taught people a method
for just letting go.

Buddhism is known for practices, like meditation, that encourage people to move beyond worldly desires, self-interests, and the attachment to permanence.

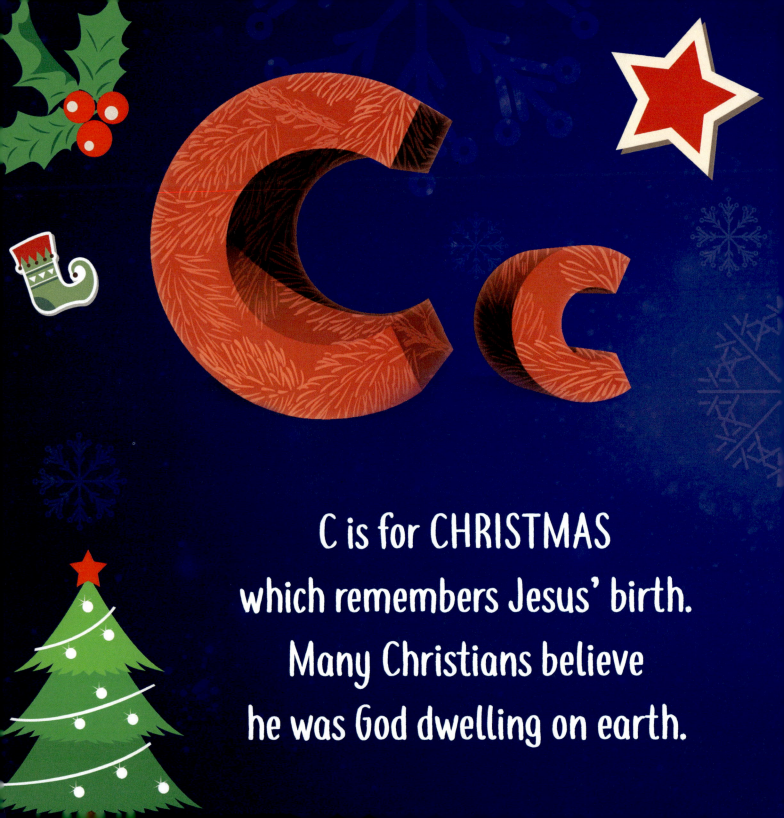

C is for CHRISTMAS
which remembers Jesus' birth.
Many Christians believe
he was God dwelling on earth.

Special births are important in several religions. Hindus, for example, observe the birth of Ganesha {guh-NESH-uh}, formed as a boy from mud before having his head replaced with that of an elephant.

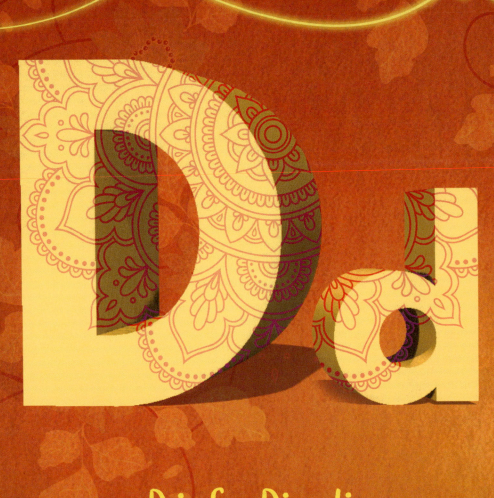

D is for Diwali,
the Festival of Lights.
Little lamps, called *diyas* {DEE-yuhs},
help to brighten the nights.

Diwali is celebrated by nearly everyone in India, including Hindus, Buddhists, Sikhs {siks}, and Jains. It celebrates the victory of light over darkness and good over evil. Hanukkah is the Jewish Festival of Lights, and Christians often talk about Jesus as the light of the world (especially at Christmas).

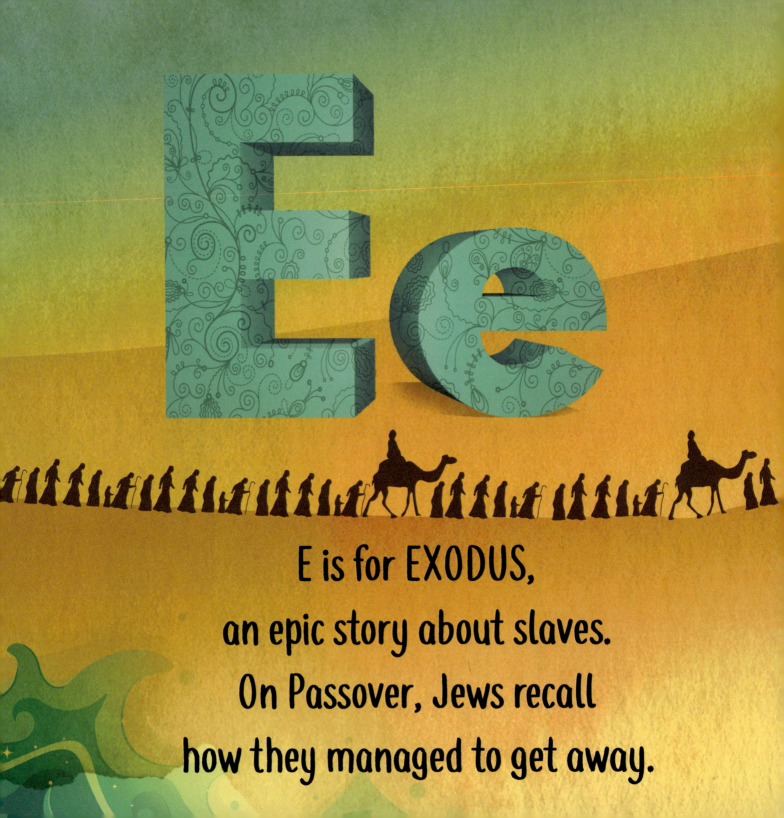

E is for EXODUS,
an epic story about slaves.
On Passover, Jews recall
how they managed to get away.

During the special meal called a *seder* {SAY-der}, Jews retell the tale of the Israelites escaping captivity. It's also used to inspire more general social justice efforts. The Exodus story is found in both the Jewish Bible and the Old Testament, so it's read by Christians, too.

F is for FASTING,
which means you don't eat.
No fruits, no veggies, no dairy,
and no meat.

Muslims observe a dawn-to-sundown fast during the month of Ramadan {RAH-muh-dahn}, Jews fast on Yom Kippur {yom kip-pur} in the fall, and Baha'is {buh-HIGHZ} fast for 19 days in the spring. Many Christians also observe either full or partial fasts during Advent and Lent.

G is for GURUS {GOO-rooz},
who are very wise teachers.
These spiritual masters
help their students think deeper.

Gurus are particularly important in the Sikh {sik} tradition which is based on the teachings of 10 human Gurus. Their sacred text, the Guru Granth Sahib {sah-heeb}, is their final Guru. Gurus are also important in Hinduism, Buddhism, and Jainism {JANE-izm}.

Muslim women always wear hijab in a mosque and some women wear hijab whenever they are in public. Head coverings, especially in sacred spaces, are also common in the Sikh tradition, for both men and women, and in the Jewish traditions, particularly for men.

I is for INDIA,
where many religions were made.
Several remain
even up to this day.

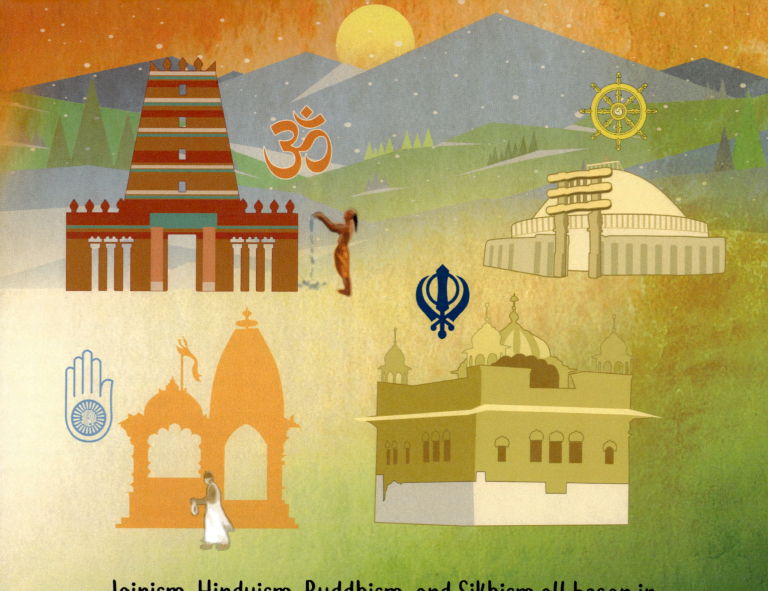

Jainism, Hinduism, Buddhism, and Sikhism all began in the southern Indus Valley, the region now called India. As a result, many rituals, concepts, practices, and holidays associated with these religions overlap.

Jj

J is for JAYANTI {jie-AHN-tee}, which means birth anniversary. They are held for gods and faith leaders who were important throughout history.

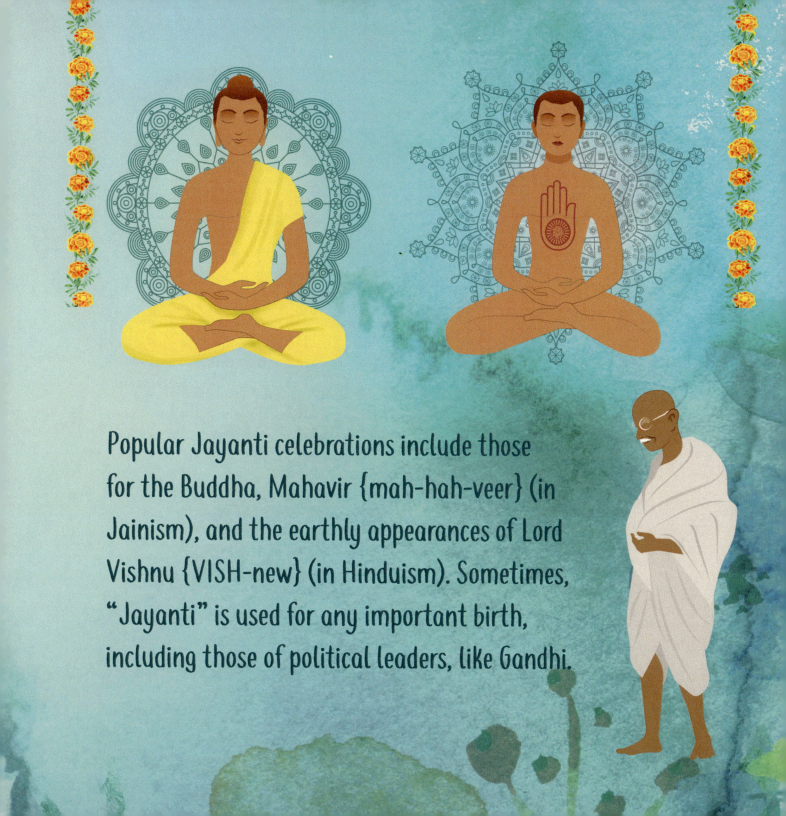

Popular Jayanti celebrations include those for the Buddha, Mahavir {mah-hah-veer} (in Jainism), and the earthly appearances of Lord Vishnu {VISH-new} (in Hinduism). Sometimes, "Jayanti" is used for any important birth, including those of political leaders, like Gandhi.

K is for KAABA {kah-bah},
Islam's most sacred site.
Visiting once in a lifetime
is a key Islamic rite.

The Kaaba is a large cube, covered with a black and gold cloth, that sits in the middle of the Great Mosque of Mecca in Saudi Arabia. During the annual pilgrimage, called the *hajj* {hahj}, Muslims walk around it seven times.

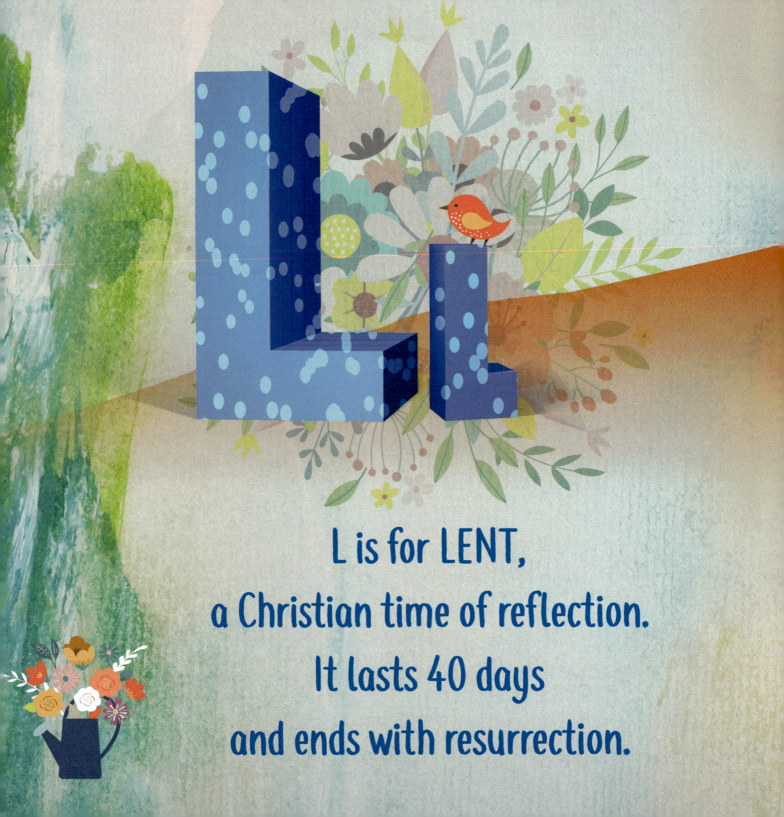

L is for LENT,
a Christian time of reflection.
It lasts 40 days
and ends with resurrection.

The Lenten period begins with Ash Wednesday (when some Christians mark themselves with ashes), goes through Good Friday (which commemorates the death of Jesus on the cross), and ends on Easter (which celebrates Jesus rising from the dead).

Mm

M is for MENORAH {meh-NOR-uh}
and the miracle of oil
when Jews reclaimed their temple
after many years of turmoil.

During Hanukkah, Jews light nine-candle menorahs to commemorate the time when a very small amount of sacred oil miraculously lasted for nine days. Non-Hanukkah menorahs, often found inside synagogues, usually have seven candles.

N is for NOBLE,
which describes the Buddha's Truths...
four important teachings
based on encounters in his youth.

When Siddhartha Gautama finally left his princely palace, he encountered the misery of sickness, old age, and death. He then spent many years identifying the true cause of suffering (desire) while outlining a path to end it (non-attachment). These central Buddhist teachings are known as the Four Noble Truths.

O is for OM,
a powerful chant for meditation.
It's simple, yet sacred,
and can aid concentration.

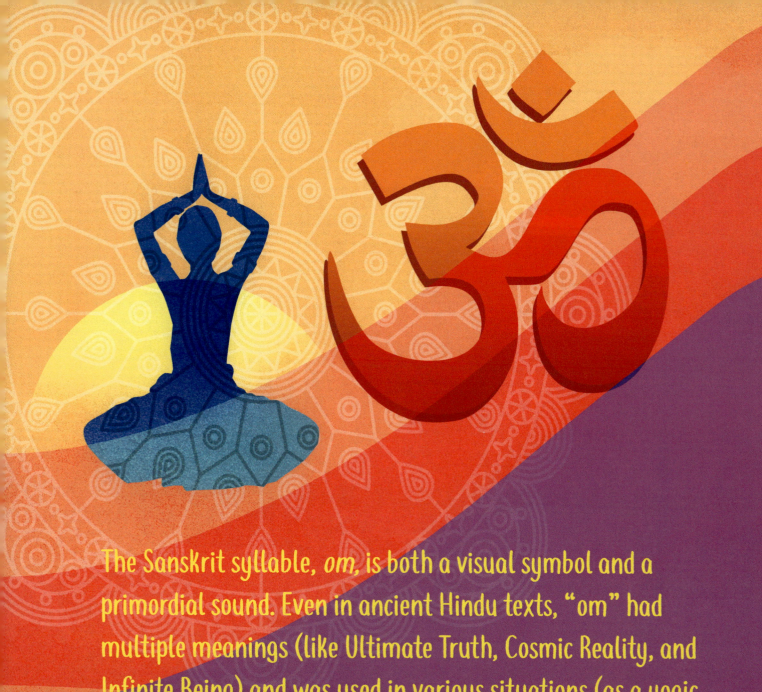

The Sanskrit syllable, *om*, is both a visual symbol and a primordial sound. Even in ancient Hindu texts, "om" had multiple meanings (like Ultimate Truth, Cosmic Reality, and Infinite Being) and was used in various situations (as a yogic mantra, in private prayer, and to consecrate rituals).

P is for PRAYER,
which comes in all forms.
Although there are guidelines,
there aren't many norms.

Prayers are found in many religious traditions — including Hinduism, Buddhism, Judaism, and Christianity — and devout Muslims pray five times a day. Prayer can include speaking aloud, thinking to one's self, meditating, or chanting. Prayer postures also vary widely.

Q is for QURAN {kur-AHN},
Islam's sacred book.
When Muslims have questions,
this is one place they look.

Most major religious traditions revere certain, historical texts. For Jews and Christians, it's some version of the Bible. For Buddhists, it's the teachings of the Buddha and his disciples. For Hindusm it's often the Vedas and the Baghavad Gita {BAH-gah-vahd GEE-tuh}.

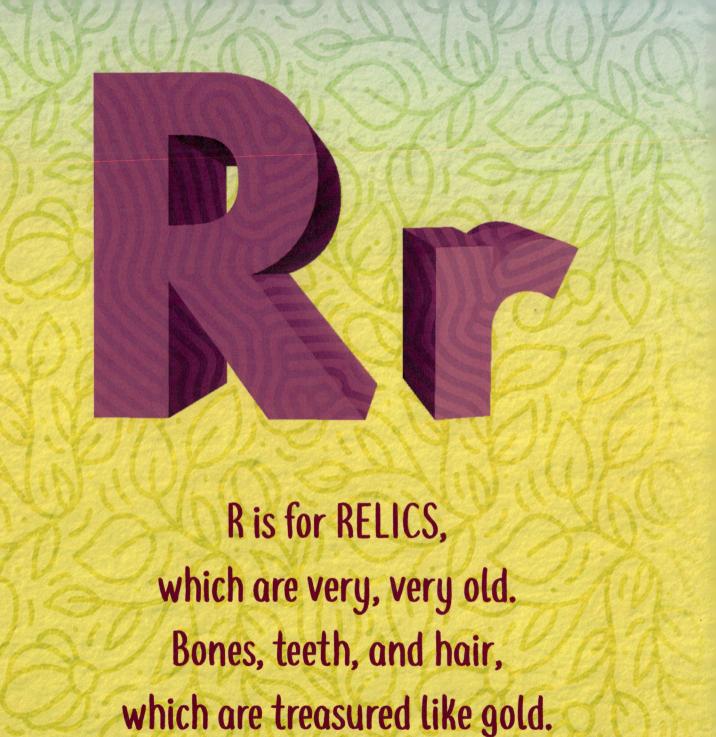

R is for RELICS,
which are very, very old.
Bones, teeth, and hair,
which are treasured like gold.

Relics, important in several traditions, are usually housed in basilicas, cathedrals, mosques, and temple complexes. They are sometimes kept in elaborately-decorated containers called reliquaries {REL-i-quare-eez} in Christianity or *stupas* {STOO-puhs} in Buddhism. Highly-respected relics serve as destinations for religious visitors, often called pilgrims.

S is for SAINTS,
whose lives we revere.
They embody compassion and love
and other qualities we hold dear.

Although called by different names in different traditions, saints demonstrate an extraordinary connection to the Divine. Saints can be male or female and, in some traditions, they are still alive. They are recognized in Hindu, Buddhist, Jewish, Islamic, Christian, and Sikh traditions.

T is for TEMPLE,
a place where groups gather,
for praying and chanting
and learning together.

All religious traditions have sacred spaces. The word "temple" is most often associated with early polytheistic traditions (like those found in ancient Egypt, Greece, and Rome), Judaism (especially the First and Second Temples of Jerusalem), Hinduism (also called *mandirs* {man-DEERZ}, and Buddhism.

U is for Unity,
which means "being one."
Acceptance of others
is one way this is done.

Religions often create boundaries between people, but knowing our neighbors — what holidays they celebrate, what special foods they eat, how they dress, and how they view the Divine Presence — helps us build bridges instead. What can you do to promote unity and harmony with the people in your community?

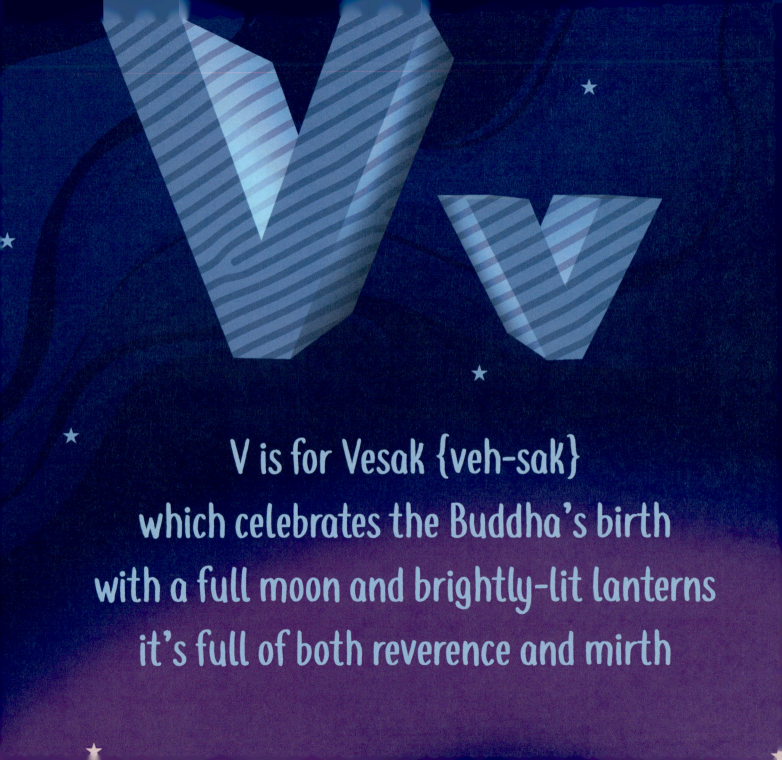

V is for Vesak {veh-sak}
which celebrates the Buddha's birth
with a full moon and brightly-lit lanterns
it's full of both reverence and mirth

In addition to parades and other performances, many Buddhists also visit temples where they meditate, listen to teachings, "bathe" Buddha statues, and make offerings of flowers or incense. Some Buddhists also commemorate the Buddha's enlightenment and death. According to tradition, all three events happened on the same full-moon day, years apart.

W starts WAHEGURU {WAH-hay-GOO-roo},
the Sikh Supreme Deity.
It means Wondrous Teacher,
existing for all eternity.

Deity names represent attempts to grasp that which is beyond our understanding. For example, Sikhs might also use *Satnam* {saht-nahm} (True Name). Jews often use Hebrew titles like *HaShem* {hah-shem} (The Name) or *Adonai* {ah-doh-NIE} (Lord). Hindus might use Brahman {BRAH-mun} (Ultimate Reality). And Muslims use Allah {ah-LAH}, the Arabic word for God.

X is for XENOS {ZEE-noce},
meaning "foreigner" in Greek,
but learning about others
should be a custom we seek.

Religious traditions, especially ones different from our own, might seem strange. But it's important to appreciate how others use their beliefs and practices to connect with the earth, the best part of themselves, and all living beings to bring greater peace and kindness to our world.

Y is for YARMULKE {YOM-uh-kuh},
the small Jewish cap
that comes in all colors.
Can you imagine that?

Most Jewish men, and many Jewish women, wear a small cap when in a synagogue. In this way, it is similar to the Sikh turban and the Islamic *hijab*. Also called a *Kippah* {KI-puh}, some Jews wear one whenever they are in public.

Z is for ZAKAT {zuh-KAHT},
which reminds Muslims to give.
Helping others is important
when they're struggling to live.

The practice of donating to those in need is found in all major religious traditions. In the Eastern traditions, it's often called *dana* {DAH-nuh}. In the Jewish traditions, it's called *tzedakah* {tze-DUCK-uh}.

A Little About Us

Rev. Vicki Michela Garlock, Ph.D. attended a Lutheran grade school (Missouri Synod), a Lutheran church (ELCA), and a Catholic high school before attending Brown University for her Sc.B. in Psychology. After earning her Ph.D. with dual specialties in neuroscience and cognitive development, she worked as a full-time psychology professor for 11 years before serving as Nurture Coordinator and Curriculum Specialist at Jubilee! Community Church. While there, she developed a Bible-based interfaith curriculum for kids and was ordained as Jubilee's Minister of Education. She currently works full-time teaching kids (and their grown-ups) about the world's faith traditions and lives her multifaith spiritual life in Asheville, NC.

Raman Bhardwaj is an international painter, muralist, illustrator, and graphic designer. Born in Chandigarh, India, he is based in Greensboro, NC. He works in both traditional and digital media. With a BFA in Applied Art and MA in Art History, Raman has been working as a professional artist since the year 2000. He has displayed in several group exhibitions in India and the U.S., and he has held solo exhibitions in India, Norway, and the U.S. In 1995, he won a national award in India for his children's book illustrations. He also won the Artpop Street Gallery award in the U.S. in 2019. Besides art, Raman has a deep interest in spirituality and Vedic Astrology.

And many thanks to Tim Hall, Ph.D., of Religion Matters (ReligionMatters.org), and Becky Michela for reviewing earlier versions of this book.

Other Books by Vicki Michela Garlock

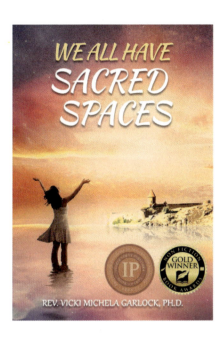

Explore the features of worship spaces in 7 different faith traditions: Indigenous, Hindu, Buddhist, Christian, Jewish, Muslim and Sikh. Photographs from around the world and questions interspersed throughout keep readers engaged. For kids age 4-10. Available on Amazon.

Gold Winner, Nonfiction Authors Association
Bronze "IPPY" Award: Multicultural Non-Fiction for Juvenile/YA
Finalist, Best Book Awards: Kids' Religious & Non-Fiction categories
Five-Star Review, Readers' Favorites

"...impressively informative and thoroughly 'kid friendly' in organization and presentation, making it an ideal and unreservedly recommended addition to family, daycare center, preschool, Sunday school, elementary school, and community library collections." *Midwest Book Review*

Every world religion encourages peace. Here, I've gathered 16 of my favorite stories from 8 different faith traditions. Each story has a full-color illustration, and the unique formatting helps kids (and adults!) learn tidbits about the world's religions while also thinking more deeply about what the narratives might mean to them.

Finalist, American Bookfest: Children's Religious
Five-Star Review, Readers' Favorites

"...I can imagine parents reading a story or two to their little ones before bed and educating them about religious tolerance from an early age. The illustrations are perfect and reflect the subject matter of the story. Well done." *Readers' Favorites*

Made in the USA
Middletown, DE
19 October 2023

40294253R00033